Curbing Your Road Rage

And Other Important Tips for Getting Along on the Road

A fun look at how we drive and behave from a Hot Head's point of view.

Library of Congress Control Number:2019915369

Dedication

To my kids, Logan and Dahlia.

To my inspiration and love, Karin Harris.

To my Mom, Dad, my sister and brother-in-law, Elisa and Bill Hirschberg and their family.

I love you.

Introduction

The process of writing this book began by laughing in the aftermath of a serious road rage episode. I was lucky it ended without a tragedy, but it frightened me. I soon realized — my rage was everywhere; it was not only present when I drove. I sent mean Tweets, put up edgy Facebook posts...have you ever been flabbergasted at a register?

 Well, who isn't ticked-off? As my Facebook news feed went by spewing political propaganda mixed with friends fighting illness, and others battling common sense, I thought, why shouldn't I be sad and angry? So, why were other people's choices and lack of driving skills making me hostile? My anger was alarming. The sadness gave me inspiration and hope.

Using the internet to express anger is easy. It's the same as lashing out at someone on the road. You're anonymous. What could be easier than directing your anger into the vastness of the web? Or, at a stranger while driving? Angry people are everywhere: online, in schools, workplaces, and — of course — on the road.

What the world needs is people willing to point their index finger at themselves and not extend their middle finger so quickly at someone else.

There is no participation trophy for buying or reading this book. But, you can give yourself a pat on the back each time you get somewhere on time, without incident, and safely. You will recognize positive change, and so will the people around you.

Acknowledge the consequences of your actions. Following angry thoughts will never take you to a happy place. Random violence inspires no one, and anyone who follows negative energy usually winds up in trouble, hurt, or dead. While you are boiling-mad, what may seem like a good idea probably isn't. We are emotional creatures with the capability to reason the unreasonable.

If you can stop yourself from writing an angry Tweet, you can steer clear of another driver on Route 66.

WHAT IS DRIVING?

Driving is controlling a vehicle through obstacles and obeying rules set down by local, state, and federal authorities. It is also a constant test of your patience resulting from other people's lack of sense and ability.

Do I even deserve keys to a car?

States should not only give a road and written test before issuing licenses, but they should also assess the mental health and anger management skills of potential drivers. Look around you. Clearly, driving tests are not a measure of one's driving ability.

The test we take now could be construed as meaningless. Many people do not drive well.

I was in a taxi, in New York City traffic when two men ran past me on the street. They stopped in front of an SUV at a red light, in front of my cab. Clearly, a traffic dispute had occurred, and the two men were there to settle it. The driver got out with a baseball bat.

I saw the wind-up, the first half of the swing, and the man walking back to his truck. After he got into his SUV, he put the bat down and drove away. As my taxi passed the injured man, his right forearm was mangled, and dangling at the point of impact.

Right then, if nothing else, I learned it is stupid to get out of your car over a traffic dispute. This incident could have gone another way – a friendly wave followed by apologetic nods and they move on like adults, the victim could have had a gun and killed the man with the bat, or his shot could have missed and killed me. If you want the keys to a car, there are many things to consider besides where you are going.

THE POWER IN KNOWING

There is real power in knowing it's your fault, and believe me, it's usually your fault.

As the operator of a motor vehicle, it is your job to be a good driver, and unless you are a driving instructor, it is not your job to teach procedure or etiquette to others. It is your job to get your car to its destination without incident or accident.

Does it matter what anyone says or writes in a book? It may! You may still overreact even though you can avoid most bad situations. Nothing will happen on the way to the pharmacy that is worth your life. Is anything worth hurting or killing your passengers?

The average person probably doesn't consider himself the aggressor. Besides, even if you have road rage, it's everyone else's fault.

Here's the thing. If you are late, it is your fault. If you don't give yourself enough time to get where you are going, it is not the fault of the person in front of you. If that person drives too slowly, it is not your fault, but it is your problem. Your problem is your responsibility. You could take your anger out on yourself, true, but somebody should at least drive the speed limit, right?

Thus began one cycle of denial, and why I kept thinking it's not my fault.

On the road, people don't seem too friendly (while not in their cars, some people ain't doing that great either). There are common reasons for unhappiness, and maybe a sense of understanding and compassion are in order?

I can't speak for your depression, hurt, fear, bitterness, loss, disappointment, wasted money (on lottery tickets alone), missed opportunities, bad breakups, self-worth, unfounded entitlement, poor choices, self-pity, or anger. So, let's talk about mine. Are we ever rid of all this anger-baggage? Can we be freed from some of the things we have in common (except you, of course)? Can the monster that lives inside us ever be squashed? Is there a time when a driver can do something idiotic, and I don't stare at them with a stupid look on my face (to show them I know they're an idiot) as I drive past them not looking forward out of my windshield, like an idiot? Anger is the root of a lot of stupidity.

So, are we squishy?

Trust me, you entitled, egotistical-narcissist – we are. My lot in life is not a result of your poor driving, it's just irritating me because it's making me late!

The only time you should lower yourself to someone else's level or below is when you're playing limbo.

Know Thy Route and Thyself

If your funeral was today, would you be in a rush to get there? Would you cut me off, and give me the finger because I was in your way? I don't think so. A grave – now, there's a place I don't want to get to first.

No, really, after you.

To be... no question.

Things ain't no big deal and just stay cool. The Fonz did not pick-up girls in high school into his forties being angry.

Stay cool. Ayyyyy!

Am I Talking To You? Wait, Reverse That!

It is hard to be a better person, and it's hard to swallow your pride. It is even harder to swallow your pride while someone is choking you.

Does this sound familiar?

You are at a light, and there is a person in a car next to you, and they have done something life-endingly unforgivable like cut you off. When you come to a stop at the next light, you hate the person driving next to you so much you'd kill them and go to jail for the rest of your life. It all makes perfect sense if you're a moron.

Then, it dawned on me. It's not everyone else whom I hate... perhaps, it is I, who needs a mirror? Maybe I should get GPS? Then I can see where I went wrong. What can I do to make my trip more enjoyable? What can I do to make life more enjoyable? Is it possible to drive somewhere with a passenger and not scare them? What happens to us in our cars that make us think we are ten feet tall and bulletproof?

I bet it's that darn rock and roll.

Why am I so angry all the time?
Get thee to a dispensary?

The Drive

We got this...

Did you hear about the Zen Buddhist who went up to a hot-dog vendor and said, "Make me One with everything?"

I am me, and you are me, and we are all in this together...

There's always that guy. The sore, bitter, angry, disappointed loser; a real jerk–the worst driver ever–a really inconsiderate low-life! Then, there's the other guy–your arch-enemy and competing reflection. A small traffic dispute and in an instant, two lives can be reduced to nothing.

If you feel like you have to tell someone off, do it so they can't see it, and say it with a foreign accent. Imitate a French, German, or an English accent. The fun of acting it out and trying a dialect should distract you, clear your mind, and put a smile on your face. Speak with an Indian, Rastafarian, or Australian accent and have fun insulting the person you wanted to yell at.

There is no need to yell at a stranger.

Say it to your dashboard. If you are not alone, share it with your passenger. You can always tell them what you are doing, and perhaps they'll join you. No need to gesture or say anything to the person in the other car. Enjoy the fact you are not upset. The other driver will be more upset that you kept your cool.

Who's our little Fonzie, now?

Buckle Up!

You may be fat, but you are not an airbag. The pine-scented paper tree air-freshener hanging from your rear-view mirror is not going to stop you from going through the windshield.

Buckle up!

Manners and Gestures

Let your fingers do the walking.

Remember, the Yellow Pages?

I don't know where I heard this, but the times they are a changin'. Now, our fingers do the texting, tapping, and picking.

IF YOU ARE PICKING YOUR NOSE IN YOUR CAR, WE CAN SEE YOU.

I once had the displeasure of looking in the rear-view mirror at a kid around twenty picking his nose repeatedly and each time, putting his finger in his mouth! I was disgusted, amazed, nauseated, and horrified.

What is wrong with people? Please research what the functions of our noses are, and you should be cured of your pick and eat disgustivity.

Pick up a book on manners and etiquette.

We already know you're good at picking things out.

Your Middle Finger

I would thrust my middle finger up in disgust, but apparently, you are ill-mannered... and legally blind?

It happens – you are driving behind someone, and they are going slow. Then you see it, a red light ahead. You know they'll probably make it through the light, and you'll be stuck there. There is nothing worse than giving them the finger and having them drive alone through that red light. You are now sitting at the light with nothing but pent-up aggression, an extended finger, and no one to share it with. Your enemy is gone, and you have to sit with yourself.

When your middle finger receives no validation, it leaves you feeling empty, maybe more angry, bitter, and definitely unfulfilled. People will drive at their own pace. Giving them the finger or throwing up your arms to provide them with a "What the hell?" Is useless. The next time this happens to you, prepare yourself to sit, instead of preparing yourself for confrontation. Better results come from better choices. How many times have you raced, darted, and sped only to be sitting at the same light as the car that never changed lanes? As my mom used to ask, "What are you rushing to? The next red light?"

Instead of one finger, put up two.
It's the difference between peace with me,

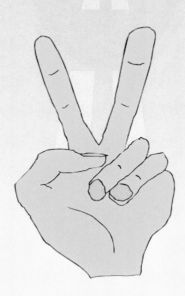

and do you want a piece of me?

Smile

Sure, going 50 miles per hour isn't bad, but remember, the other guy is probably doing 50 also. Hitting a wall at 50 miles per hour is not good and hitting a wall at 100 miles per hour is doubly not good. I'll leave it at that.

Smile.

People will identify with your smile.

If you drive too fast, they may have to identify you by your dental records.

Pulling Out and Tailgating

They are much more fun in bed.

I shoulda been somewhere. I coulda ruined my fender.

No one knows you are in a rush. Having extra space between you and the car in front of you can prevent automatic and instant anguish. It can stop you from doing everything stupid does. **Yes, just by being too close.**

When I am angry tailgating, I connect to the car in front of me with negative energy and a physical force. As I get closer to its fender, I focus more intensely, and my adrenaline builds.

Having space between your car and the car in front of you, allows you to breathe and have a safe zone by not attaching yourself, in any way, to the vehicle in front of you.

I used to get annoyed when a driver would pull out abruptly and cut me off. My 38 miles per hour becomes 24 miles per hour, and I would tailgate, so they knew it. A simple (and more useful) approach is to slow down and keep a greater distance between the car that just sparked my tizzy, and me.

It took me a try or seven to do it. As I did, you may find yourself automatically getting less aggressive. When you are angry, do not tailgate, it is easy to get the other driver angry, too.

Save your tailgating for sporting events.

The Left Lane

With my girlfriend seated beside me, I was driving 65 miles per hour on a highway. We approached a car going 50 miles per hour in the left lane. I was incredibly patient for what seemed like hours, and after those four seconds were over, I flashed my brights for the old man to get out of my way. Instead of moving over when he could, he jammed on his breaks, and I almost hit his car from behind. I lost my proverbial mind. I was screaming and gesticulating and doing that thing where you grab your steering wheel and shake your hands back-and-forth with all your might and scream while trying to pull it off of the steering column (because you don't need a steering wheel to drive).

I got in front of him and brought the traffic to 4 miles per hour in the left lane of a highway so I could try to get out of a moving car and attempt murder. Luckily, I looked over to my right – my girlfriend was in tears, and I immediately stopped what I was doing.

I had disregarded her thoughts and feelings, what she was experiencing, and her fear of dying. I got so blinded by my rage, I forgot she was even in the car. If someone chooses to yell at you and flip you off, let them. Wave and say, "I'm sorry." It's no guarantee you'll avoid trouble, and allowing an idiot to

think they're right is not a big deal. Wave and let them go on their grumpy way. Time spent messing around in a hostile situation will further postpone your arrival time. It's called karma, and one day they will do something selfish or stupid to the wrong person. Your day is not more important than mine. If there is an exit, don't be a pig–get in the designated exit line and wait like everyone else. It's selfish to drive up and cut people off. Once, I was on an exit ramp, I watched a man open his door and say something to the driver, now behind him, that he didn't let in front of him, at the last minute. Have you ever been delighted someone wasn't talking to you? *I have.*

If somebody comes speeding up behind you quickly in the left lane, let them pass. Don't speed up as they try to pass you.

Let them go and be happy. It doesn't matter, and it will probably be the only time in life they will be ahead of you.

Alternate Merge

When you say alternate, do you mean every other?

Yes. Here, have a hot-dog.

Look Ma, I'm alternating.

Depending on your location, you have to be courteously aggressive to drive, or you may never get anywhere. But when there is a situation requiring a simple, alternate merge, just do it.

Yes, you think your life is more important than everyone else's, but remember, all of us are created equal. Wait for your turn.

One day, I was in an alternate merge situation, the driver behind the car who just merged, decided that instead of letting me go next, he was going cut ahead of me. As we both tried to merge in the same spot, I heard the awful sound of metal hitting metal, and I knew our vehicles had become intimate.

Because of karma (I can't explain why), his truck was torn-up in front, and I had no damage to my car. He keeps insisting that it's my fault and begins to get in my face as a policeman drives up. The officer asked if we needed anything, and I gestured to the person unable to figure out alternate merge. He smiled and said, "No." I wished everyone well, got in my car, and drove away in front of him, behind the cop, in my proper place.

Alternate merge means every other. *If you are looking to screw someone in a merger, go to business school.*

Prison

Having a personalized license plate can be cool, but making one is not. You don't want to die in a road rage fight, but how about doing the killing? I knew a guy who served two years for killing someone in a bar fight he didn't start. Do you have two years to spend in jail for being right?

Having a roommate can be okay, but it's much nicer having a roommate the state didn't choose.

Sing!

Radio Killed The Novella Star

Just sing, sing a song. Forget about everyone else and make it loud, perhaps strong. Do it, even if you think you sound bad, or if you think you're not good enough.

Singing is good for the heart and soul. You may be off-key, but if you are in the moment, your ex could cut in front of you, and you'd wave and smile. Roll up your windows if you have stage fright, or you really don't want people to hear you sing. They don't matter. It's for you, anyway.

WIGGLE YOUR WAY OUT OF IT

Are you tired of listening to news and politics? A drive with just your thoughts is fantastic; otherwise, your radio can keep you cool.

If you bet on sports, don't listen to the game while you are driving. Put on music you like.

I recommend Deuter, Andreas Vollenweider, any mellow classical pieces, or any artist who produces peaceful music.

Try music with no lyrics and don't be afraid of any thoughts you may encounter. It could lead to another thought and the next thing you know you could be on your way to being civilized. Music and movies are not to blame for your bad attitude, you are. If you are violent, it is not the fault of thrash metal.

If you can't find music that soothes you, put on kid's music like the Wiggles or Laurie Berkner – it's harder to get mad at somebody when you're singing Fruit Salad, Victor Vito, or Rocketship Run.

Blaming music, or art for violence is like blaming the crash of the Hindenburg on Led Zeppelin, but it can't hurt when trying to maintain a calm disposition.

There is something about driving in your car that instantly gives you the ability to be a moron and an inability to see it happen. You must take control of your own actions, and what you are hearing and singing can pleasantly decorate your space.

If your sports team sucks, do not listen to the game while you drive!

Brights

While operating a motor vehicle, out of the five senses we have, sight is the most important.

Turn your brights off in two way traffic.

Electronic Toll Readers

If you live in an area with an automated toll system, sign up. It will speed up your trip, and it will improve your attitude.

Then, you can drive by all those people in line at a toll and say, "How can you not have a freakin' electronic toll pass?"

Guns Don't Kill People

Yes, they do.

Who's on first?

Death.

Third base.

US Representatives were shot at and hurt playing baseball. Do you remember when baseball had the rundown and not the gun down? In this country, only our tolerance, politics, manners, respect, and education can be worse than our aim.

Nobody likes to be shot at even if they are wrong. Some of us think we live in the Wild West. Unless you've galloped on horseback to your saloon while uttering through chaw, "This town ain't big enough for the two of us," put your guns down.

Shoot at the range, not at people in range.

Therapy

Watching Dr. Phil does not constitute therapy.

Did you hear the one about the Zen Buddhist ordering a hot dog?

If you can't control your anger, seek professional help. This is not a book telling you to let everyone go in front of you and wave. I know you have to be aggressive to drive in a city, I grew up driving in New York City. I understand which lane to be in for the fastest route cross-town, how to cut off a cop, and not see the woman with the stroller next to the Vespa. While city driving may involve aggressive driving, it doesn't mean you can't remain calm.

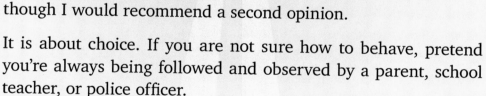

If you think you are touching base with your inner self by watching somebody like Dr. Phil or becoming wiser by Dr. Oz, that's great, I am not going to dispute your progress though I would recommend a second opinion.

It is about choice. If you are not sure how to behave, pretend you're always being followed and observed by a parent, school teacher, or police officer.

Breathe deeply and let it all go. It is not a failure to admit you need help and then get it – it is a failure not to.

Couch Mouth

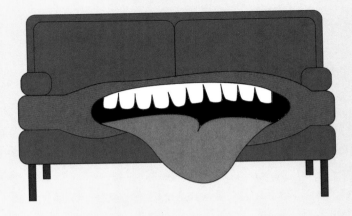

You're always on a couch, therapy takes place on one, and that is a beautiful start.*

*If your couch involves a video game controller or an episode of Law and Order, it's probably the wrong couch.

If you're having anger management issues, welcome to the world. There are common problems that may cause you distress such as owing money, being in a lousy relationship, kids drive you nuts (and they're expensive), you can't study, and you can't work.

Your mind is filled with ideas, "I think my boss is so dumb, and he is such a jerk! I'm under-appreciated underpaid, and under-laid. Everything sucks. I am so out of shape, I pulled a muscle running to the bathroom. Things are horrible, especially at this very moment!"

Now, add somebody else's lousy driving into this toxic mix. Someone you can blame. People can be mad at themselves and not at you.

They may not realize it, so they may take it out on you. People need a lot of things; therapy, medication, and true company are a few. You never need to put up your middle finger.

A random, off-the-cuff gesture could be what sets somebody off – don't give them a reason. I know, you're tough, MMA tough – we all get it.

Maybe your loved ones aren't as tough? Who wants to cry at your funeral because you couldn't let some psycho get in front of you without giving him the finger?

Be Nice, You #%@!

Are you talking to you?

Am I talking to me?

I was driving in bumper to bumper traffic. Someone who wanted to change lanes put on his blinker, and in my delusion, I waved and let him in. In this long line of traffic, I was shocked anything could make me feel good. Then, it dawned on me. I don't have to be a jerk. If I let someone in, they may even wave thank you. It's actual communication as if I am not the only one on the planet. You know what I hate? I do something nice and those self-righteous people can't even lift up a hand to wave and say thank you. How hard is it? I hate that. I just let you in… you selfish…

Oh, what? I mean, I am so sorry… Cuddles, your dog just died! I'll cut you some slack. Please, after you.

Or maybe cousin Vinny just failed the bar exam, again. Or maybe they're just spacing out, thinking about…oh, I dunno…

Or perhaps they just could use a break? Please, go ahead.

Didn't you ever feel like you could use a break from being angry?

The trick is to stay on that break.

Nothing worthwhile is easy but remember this – it takes more muscles to frown than it does to smile.

Blinkers

Your blinker is not a pacemaker – you can turn it off. Obviously, I am talking about your blinker. The way you drive, it seems you've already turned off your pacemaker.

If your blinkers do not work, get them fixed. If they do work, please use them. Other drivers should be alerted to your car's activity. Turning, pulling out, or changing lanes requires a tiny bit of extra effort and is a simple consideration.

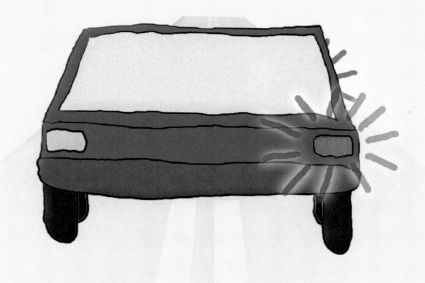

Drinking, Drugs, and Driving

Drinking, drugs, and driving do not work. It is illegal, stupid, and deadly. If you're out, the same drink that told you that you can dance should have also told you not to drive. If you think it's okay to smoke pot and drive, you are already high, it's not. Hey! Over here! Hello! It's not. Ugh! It's not okay to smoke pot and drive! Never mind. Here's a Slinky, go play on the stairs.

If you kill somebody while you are driving wasted, the prison sentence following your DUI will be the better part of your life, if not all of it.

Chances are, you don't have what it takes to survive in prison if you are there by accident.

Also, you are not important enough to kill anyone.

Making a Left Turn

If you are making a left turn, please move over to the left side of the lane! Others would like to get by you on the right – there is usually enough room.

If you are making a left, do not turn the wheels of your car until you are ready to turn. Keep your tires straight. If someone rear-ends you, and you have already begun to make your turn, you could be rear-ended into oncoming traffic.

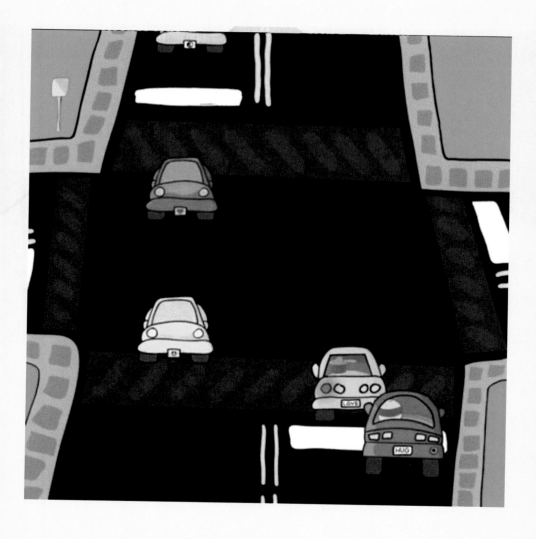

Lost and Found

Ask any kid under 21 who Rand McNally was, and if they have remotely heard of *them*, they'll probably think they helped program Google Maps.

With the advent of GPS on our phones, the days of needing to stop at gas stations for maps and directions are long gone. In short, men have spent decades not wanting to take directions from women. Now? They buy a GPS device and have a woman's voice tell them what to do and where to go at every turn. Use common sense and ask for directions.

Possibly feeling a little foolish is better than being a lost fool.

The Phone

Put the phone away while you are driving. I guarantee you, your texts are not an important enough reason to kill somebody, or yourself. What's more important, controlling a multi-thousand-pound vehicle safely, or calling your office?

I give my phone to my kids while I drive, and I let them pick songs to play.

You are still not important enough to kill someone. Nobody is.

Put the phone down while you are driving.

NO EXCEPTIONS!

While this is a book about driving and our collective attitudes, don't think because you wave and you're a good person, someone else isn't nuts. Dial 9-1-1, and let authorities handle a person who is overreacting, or freaking out. Their parents couldn't handle them, how can you?

Most cars can dial a phone by voice or a button on the steering wheel. If not, and you can't pullover to dial 9-1-1, that should be the only time your phone is in your hand while you are driving. ***Seriously!***

Parking

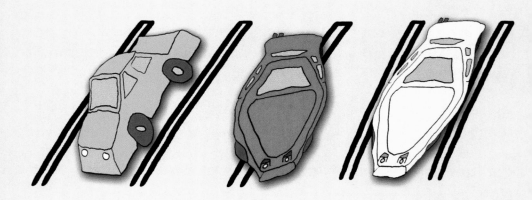

Even if you can't read between the lines, you can still park between them.

When someone's car takes up two spots, so no one damages it, that makes people want to damage it.

Arriving!

EVERYONE HERE GETS OUT ALIVE

Take the Break!

 Everybody has a bad day, and while today may not be yours, it may be one for the person next to you. Let someone deal with their vet's news, a sick spouse, or a job loss. The sweetest person in the entire world could be in the car that just didn't wave thank you. They could have something else on their mind. Take a break.

If you don't want a break, give someone else a break. The best thing to do is to remember you are in control. It is your job to get your car to its destination, without incident or accident. The trip can be a pleasant one. It is up to you.

Put the phone down – it doesn't matter if you just got dumped and have to keep checking your messages every 30 seconds in case the object of your affection decides to text. Do you know what will be on Facebook? "Charlie died when his car hit a tree while reading a text from his ex saying she wants him back. The funeral is set for Wednesday."

Will Attend or Will Not Attend?

Take a breath, slow down, relax, put the phone down, and everyone here will get out alive.

Give yourself and the rest of us a break…

Come on, we've got this.

Tips for Thought

PUT THE PHONE DOWN

GAPS IN TRAFFIC, CAUSE TRAFFIC: KEEP UP

PARK YOUR CAR IN 1 SPOT

DON'T TAKE 10 MINUTES TO PULL OUT OF A PARKING SPOT IF SOMEONE IS WAITING

PUT THE PHONE DOWN

DON'T DRINK AND DRIVE

KEEP ALL GESTURES TO WAVING

THERE IS A TWO FINGER MINIMUM

LET A JERK GO IN FRONT OF YOU

PUT THE PHONE DOWN

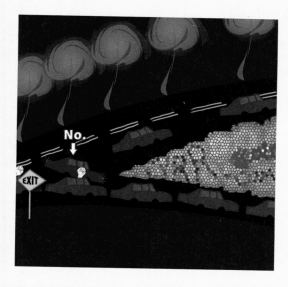

DON'T CUT PEOPLE OFF AT EXIT RAMPS WHO HAVE BEEN WAITING TO EXIT

YOU DON'T HAVE TO BE RIGHT

LET SOMEONE GO IN FRONT OF YOU

PUT THE PHONE DOWN

DON'T HONK AS SOON AS THE LIGHT TURNS GREEN

IT'S YOUR FAULT YOU'RE LATE

DRIVE THE SPEED LIMIT, OR PULLOVER SO WE CAN

IT'S CALLED ALTERNATE MERGE, FOR A REASON

IF SOMEONE IS PASSING YOU, DON'T SPEED UP

PUT THE PHONE DOWN

AND GET OUT OF THE LEFT LANE!

To Julia, Lauren, and James Hirschberg.

To: Michael Rogers, Steven Rudolph, Pablo Francisco, Mat Becker, Steven Scott, Doug Stanhope, Bobby Collins, Jennifer Star, Gil Altman, Ipar L'Aimable, Bev West, Billee Howard, Lauren Verge, Stephani Astolfi, Mary and Dave Kupferschmid, Gayle and Mel Gerstein, Bonnie and Ben Greenberg, Heather Gornall, Mike Nasr and Sheridan Burrage, Christian Sandoval, and my other three girls Samantha, Baylie, and Remi Harris.

About the author: Gordon Feinberg was born in New York City and raised in northern New Jersey. As a middle-aged man with an ex-wife, two kids, and a driver's license, he knows all about getting angry. Gordon is a graduate of Northeastern University and has been a graphic designer for more than thirty years. His hobbies include music, acting, stand up comedy, ice hockey, writing, drawing, and animation.

Thanks!

Made in the USA
Middletown, DE
12 August 2022